# FACES OF MY PHASES

## YOGESH KARKI

Made with ❤ on the Notion Press Platform
www.notionpress.com

.

*to one of the phases*

# Contents

# Contents

# Acknowledgements

*Firstly, I would like to thank all my friends who read the poems I posted throughout the years and helped me improve in my initial years, either directly or indirectly.*

Endless thanks to my sister Neha for encouraging this poetry thing all along. My mother, for whom I occasionally have to translate every line.Haha, more love to her and my father for always being supportive.

Thank you to the newspapers, magazines, schoolbooks, and teachers, especially Mrs. Monika Mam and Mrs. Gayatri Chand Mam, who sparked my interest in poetry and everything.

I can offer no amount of thanks whatsoever to my favourite Mrs. M.K. Singh Mam for guiding me through my worst years and being the only one to believe in me when no one else did.

Also, I can't name them all, but whoever followed my poetry page that goes by @05_a_cursed_love_10 on Instagram helped me a lot by making me believe that there is someone out there who feels and can relate, and by making me believe that my work is worth reading and publishing.

*A special shoutout to Shreyash Bro for the amazing book cover artwork!*

Finally, to those people in my life who have caused me to go through bad phases—people who never listened, who left unexpectedly, who made me feel irrelevant in my most desperate moment, and who eventually made writing my emotions out through poetry an escape mechanism—I bear no grudges, and I thank you for inspiring me to be FACES OF MY PHASE-1.

*Also, I would be very thankful to all the new readers; the more, the better.*

# 1. where it all started..

# affinity and blight

*my poetry says a lot about you*
*marks in the sand of memory, leaving no clue*
*options are many, but not willing to choose*
*sorry it's the trust that I always lose*

*and never asked for a relationship;*
*but a love that ends in infinity*

**nothing but a cursed_love's affinity**

*hands so tight; still feels so low*
*being in my mind upright;*
*untrusted thoughts would blow*
*seemed out of my sight;*
*keep vanishing in my sand's snow*

*hoping we would shut up and grow*

*remembering the trust deeds;*
*that we would complete*
*on the funeral of our feeling's fleet;*

*with a smiling greet and flow*

*came into my love's limelight would hold you and cry for a while*
*we're still friends that won't bite*
**my cursed_love -The Biggest Blight**

# only regret

*priorities that we should get*
*now even best friends neglect*
*they say we're grown up*
*not even a teardrop to show up*
*but eventually, they get underground*
**messy issues with cursed_love fucking around**

*sometimes it's a choice I regret*
*exceptional cases made me forget*
*clear in mind cheerful those days*
*depressed mind still prays*

*memories to go back to neither of you*
*it was mine that I thought about you*
*portals to my heaven of anxiety*
**in first place doors of it carved by you**

*angst was ugly but real; last said things would clear*
*hoping for the best amongst the worst*
**being hopeful is only regret that I fear**

# installing the mood

*installing the mood we prefer;*
**for the first time**

*showing I always do care;*
*making relations worth bright*

*we talk about topics;*
*none care to be judged*

*sometimes about personal misery;*
*to an extent, I can take and be tough*

*not expressing the problems I face;*
*even though the immense trust we embrace*

*letting someone into my thought process*

*not what I easily let them through, my grace*

**would we rather be the same?**

*scratching through rough bare hand*

*hurting the empty space you found;*
**another reason to leash our demons' crowd**

# the Reason

**okay, so again, you**
*just some things that were left unsaid*
*yeah, I told you I'd already moved on*
*not just from you and your city*
*but somewhat with my own*
*obsessiveness towards you and self-pity*

*I still love you, as always done*
*I still adore you the same way before*
*I still observe you and learn*
**ways not to give a damn anymore**

*we can't, but I talk to you in real*
*you sit right beside me, just near*
*with hands tied and talk for hours with no fear*
*can hear your voice still, profound and clear*

**I still wish you last on your birthday**

*just a few seconds before it ends*
*to tell~ with you till the end;*

*no matter what will be our future*
*or what we would grow up to be*
*if anyone asks you about me*
*and the success of this literature*

*proudly tell them you are the REASON*

# reinitiation

*the broken pieces that you left*
*not even knowing the worst end*
*promise you owed wasn't heard*
**justification through tears was a bit weird**

*we should not get trapped in a relationship, you say*
*seen carving out my heart & mind like clay and left dry*
*leaving my part & side not giving 13 reasons why*

**is there someone who can feel**
*waiting for love that would heal*

*the wounds of fake love she would feel*
*now trust bandages won't heal*
**having inexact follow-up to train**
*hope you understand the same*

*then decide what obsessiveness I endure*
*the sufferings of trust that she caused*
*a beautiful heart to be regretful and lost*

*lame thoughts came up with my feelings*
**procurement of dumb luck would do further healing**

# she asked though

*-She asked though*

*secrets we don't ask for, so-called trust blowed*
*still the same lesson, when would we grow?*

*feeling something less than nothing*
*Your mistake, though! why me to bow?*

*misconceptions on the hypersomnia road*
*believe my self-made conspiracy to some extent*

*She asked though*

*missing a happening to mishappening of an event's row*
*already being active, passive, you don't*

*Choosing the easy words; vocabulary you would understand*
*rhyming scheme still messed up, references to you still get tough*

*-She asked though*

*for the millionth time not to overthink*
*all these insecurities would not uplift*

*the diverse character that I possess*
*multiple personalities with a big*
*management errors*

*Hope you get to know me well; the personality in front of you i prefer*

**She asked though**

sorry to begin, or a sorry to end

the mood shattered (?) being over possessed (!)


I think it would make sense; calling out a name I don't understand

still talking about them from the day start

to a

sorrowful end...

# we kids!

***we kids!** yeah! we 21^st^-century kids wannabe billionaires to be wealthy rich*

*scrolling through motivational pages without hustling in real life; not doing a thing*

*to make it happen but dreaming about giving a privileged life to our future*

*wannabe at the job before turning 25; competing with fellows throughout the life*

*is this all meaningless maybe yes, maybe not. who knows what we will get?*

*out of all this shite we are all going through or the mental issues we are recovering from,*

*will it pay back as it seems to be just hoping to some extent you only know the truth*

*are you doing enough to make your dreams come true? give yourself a review*

*escaping from all your problems! or trying to find wisdom teeth gums!*


*__or are you from the privileged ones!__ who already got out of this whole hustling burns*

*big cars! good outfits! the easy path laid out for your career, but what 'bout the growth?*

*soaked up in the bathtubs, and with no financial problems in hand, skin as soft as rose*

*bare hands, never done hard work before, and making others feel inferior by the stories that you post*

*__or are you the rebellious one__ who wanna start everything from scratch*

*and wanna do it all by yourself; not giving a damn about what people would say about the way that keep you going or backup that you don't have; throughout*

*the day*

*putting work back and forth results are still the same, the time you gave to pray*

*for getting eaten up as capitalism's prey?* **controlling grudges is enough brave**

# depressed days?

*depressed days are the days*
*when the best finds himself at worst*
*not only within but tries to find flaws*
**in his actions that put not worth**


*hard to digest any of our great work at that time;*
*being pessimistic all the time*
*starts to find alternative steps*
*that might have been taken or done*
**looping a particular event or period that was fun;**
*and whining*


*about it all the night again and again that when we would learn;*
*and stop diving*
*in with the great skeptic nature we build on;*
*trusting nobody to tell about this all*
*thinking their nature toward us will eventually fall*
**or they will judge for not being man-up;**


**and just**
*pass the days by keeping your mouth shut*
*or they will always treat you like the depressed kind*
*and just escaping to nowhere where no one can find*
*both of you: you and your story behind it*

*not telling this to the close ones and telling them to avoid it*
**like it never happened and you only experienced a little bit**


*like I know I got many problems from which I even don't know their names*
*escaping through insomniac problems by playing games*
*days and nights for just the fight you will do with your eyes*
*to please sleep and not act so weird or creepy*
*running out of words not pain to fill in*
*enough of my blames and causes to dig in*
**lastly promising not to overthink the anxiety**
**wishing there were bigger plans just for you, by the almighty**


**build up enough courage and be enough brave**
**depressing about depression might end up in grave**

# apart from being broke

*apart from being broke,*
**_what you gotta say(?)_**
*innocence of her duke;*
*that made you prey?*
*or marrying in her dreams.*
*as you always pray?*
*not believing someone;*
*sacrifice you would pay?*
*not gonna lie but Forgot*
*she would betray*
*nice! still listening to her*
*problems you wanna say?*
*stressing about stress;*
*though! sleep finds the way?*
*apart from being broke,*
**_what you gotta say?_**

# went down to write

*went down to write*
*issues already arrived*

**difficulty to choose**
*hard to knowingly remove*

*though just like you*
*the crazy relationship we brew*

**not giving a goddamn clue**
*rolling up with anxiety's crew*
*this crew holds some alumni*
*of mine*
*grown up with days of dry*

*mercy in the devil's cry*
*bribe for the fame we thrive*
**be a man, be enough brave**
*start to*
**settle out depression's grave**

*nothing about give and take dumbfuck face*
*still feels the same*

**pen down to the further ache**
*one more time*
**for my sake**

# 2. maybe i'm not what you dreamed..

# maybe

***maybe we were meant to be***, *totally different and not worthy*
*of couple goals that we seek; or the mercy on us that we plead*
*through all these years of deep and leftover jealousy*
*might sound uncanny but true about boredom's seed*
*that I only sow but do not reap..*


***maybe we could trust and regret it later; a lot goes through***
*mind's inside, overcome the bigger fears to show*
*It's nothing but a daydream without the sun's glow*
*could doubt and regret later to the deep end*
*it would send to settle the dues or to begin..*


***maybe we could draw a silver lining to our relationship and leave it***
***unnamed***
*for a while till we decide on a name for the untamed*
*always allied to you but never lied to you; and never ashamed*
*of the past, we did wrong or the things that debt*
*unsaid for sure or sheer anxiety to get*
*rather set to endure together what's left*


***maybe we aren't, but remember***
*at least*
*we simply meant to be "together & forever"*

as I dreamed

# i'm

**I'm**

*that note you kept aside and reopened sometimes*
*but never tried to write on it again in life*
*maybe for the better, great, and thrive*
*in a better way to stick to it and redefine*

**I'm**

*that playlist you saved for the saddest time*
**chastised for owning deceptive grinds**
*but I know I will guide you till the end*
*Remember, I gave you the name "Lian Nishang."*
*back then?..*

**I'm**

*that golden timetable you always want to be followed*
*but never did, trembled at your superiority*
*or maybe out of my inferior complexity*
*or the narcissistic attitude you showed, which I swallowed and threw*

**I'm**

*that journal to keep up with prioritised tasks*
*not check marked till end of this day*
*but I'm sure you would be regretted in yourself and pray*
*to give it a try or a chance to new one that lasts*

**I'm**

*that success that you love*

*without enduring the path's pain*
*with you without shame*
*always handling you with kid gloves*

**I'm**

*bleeding from here and there*
*from eyes or from different pens*

**ignore this as always in all ways**
**if it doesn't make any sense.**

# not

*Not said to take care; before sleep*
*or sweet dreams to share; might end up in grief*
*not too hard to bear; acting completely freak*
*missing existence, wishing I wouldn't leave*


*Would be someone to care about; someone there to fear*
*the platform we summarize our day in brief*
**might be a little dumbfuck, but acting mature**
**sometimes this dumb still fucks up for sure**
*recovery from being numb already got the cure*
**just to lie beside my mum, just to reassure**


*from how things would go and how it end up there*
*still, that immature chum that is still insecure*
*The void you left before only needs you to fill-up*
**End up being bored; my feelings! Storm in a teacup?**


*shutting down the door to everybody might be some rough*
*of the pain that I endure that won't cough up*
*even to my best friends who don't know how to care*
**Procrastination isn't pure, but I know my damn luck**

# what

*what's the point of being hard all the time?*

*or being stressed over enough validation*

*that should be but isn't provided by*

**Are they afraid to connect my name with theirs?**

*all the time*


*Maybe correct because I haven't gotten there yet*

*like a model's face or good pictures to show them*

*or work that's worth sharing*

*or a superiority that's worth caring*

*or popularity by doing something daring*

*what's the point if I don't get that?*

*haunting complexities would get back*


*what if someday there will be this point*

*that will answer all my miseries of past*

*but what's the benefit of that point?*

*that not even passed*

*without the regret of letting it go*

*in whichever way it goes*

*from the friend or to the foes to scratch my*

*head to toe of the anxiety that grows*

*that wasn't solved by the dose of smile that I got*

*to show others;* **still, there were parts to part ways for**

*what's the point in being the badass to prove*
*or being a nice guy that finishes last*
*Is that bad? to finish last?*
*At least I finished; we should be together*
**someday we will give it another chance**
**we would say;**

*what if, that day, I breathe out and die?*
*I'm sure we will live in an afterlife*
*that's absurd, but now we got time*
*to talk with the almighty*
*about the fate that he laid on us*

**He would say:**
**"you already named it**
**and that's your a_cursed_love"**
*would be enough to hush...*

# you

**you are that much into my poetry**
*now I think of you in rhymes*
*I describe you under the same tree*
*of unrequited love fate crimes.*


**you are the best metaphor for my lines**
*always counted you as my liberty*
*to stride into the room at times*
*of biting my nails and talking freely.*


**you are like phrases to phases of my life**
*incomplete, but have some meaning inside*
*for the expression to be wise and nice*
*to what that's ineffable to my mind,*
*you are kinda deafening sound*
*especially to my brain's cloud; a soothing voice I'm listening*
*of some relatable singer that loud*


**you are into every other atomic habit I pick,**
*A new one is to put a diary beside my pillow*
*If I think about us again, a fast scheme*
*the brain to take some notes in the nightmare's flow*
*every time..*

# dreamed

**as a child, I used to dream a lot**
*about my companions being together in the rain*
*to the end of life's drought*
*they flew like hairs in a feather without pain*
*just realised they were never knot*
*properly and bought myself some same*
*and instant regret in the game,* **plus the vain**


*never dreamed of this existential pressure*
*back then and never questioned the reality*
*shown by others and no curiosity to share*
**a byproduct of gaining some extra layers**
*was the thing that made me empty*
*before filling it completely*


*dreamed about you and me sharing the same fate*
*to an extent that seemed true but blurred*
**together and forever goals for selfish sake**
*that was meant to be met as an adult*
*was best for the character development*
*not that sad about the sorrowful end*


*dreamed your name on my* **epitaph of**

*understanding*; sort of generation gap
now fixating on it being dark black
nothing is written on its front or back
end of our concept of love that lack


**as a child, I used to dream a lot**
and scream out of joy that will be brought
but I'm sure
it's not even one percent that I dreamed
found relatable therapy lessons to the core
that we feel exhausted but good when screamed...

# 3. where it took a pause and resumed frequently..

# simile

**Breath**

*It's always the one who takes away*

*not the one who lets you*

*It's raining outside*

*and the first thing that came into my head*

*is to call my best friend*

**she adores rain just like me**

*I enjoy it in my bed,*

*she enjoys it to the day's end*

*I didn't enjoy it until we met.*


*she runs, jumps, laugh*

*with wide-open arms*

*and giggles*

*to whatever I say,*

*which was hushed in half*

*by heavenly droplets that fell*

*to my face and her ears at*


**will thank the selfish clouds**

*that suck up from one source*

*and don't pour it*

*in the same poor doors*

***DOES HE THINK THERE IS NO NEED?***

*I don't know what to believe*
*but I believe it was meant for us*
*something like a takeaway by upper ones*
*and the joy of a giveaway*
*in her & my face for once*
*which I'm sure would last for days*
*will sing the song of praise*
**be a bee in one's bonnet as a grace**


*you told me to keep*
*the last lines are unchanged*
*so here it is, as it should be:*
**the first time she was in a rush**
**Next time, we would**
**smell the same soil's dust,**
**and drown in every feeling we could**
**a sing a song we dedicated to each other**
**without the exact lyrics to bother**

# it would be simple

**Yeah, it would be simple if**

I'd give fewer fucks

to everything that happens

to everything that messes up

*to those who don't prioritise me*


***It would be simple but isn't***

*people would not rely on luck*

*to meet a soulmate at a drastic end*

*to meet the mate that looks them up*

*to both good and bad times and not flee*


***It would be simple if***

*I would not become numb*

*every time saw you face to face*

*every time start venting about a lot*

*every time strangers laughed*


***It would be simple if***

*people wouldn't be dumb*

*to think they can find every trace*

*to someone's processing of thought*

*to correct what they only dwarfed*

**it would be simple but isn't**
Not everybody wants a change within
but want in others for sure
just an eternal curse deep in
which has precautions, but no cure..

# upcoming success

**probably won't**

*I won't call you mine, especially this time*
*when I am doing my best, ignoring the rest*
*past that gone depressed, with only some regrets*
*with all my mates; fake friends gone at impressive rates*

**Yes, I don't remember dates, even the special ones**

*but I remember the event that took place*
*in my face with the days dark;* **lived with open burns**
*normalise not celebrating birthdays; enjoying your existence?*
*or just pretending in various ways; like me just in terms*
*living at a delusional level of happiness and presence*
*of impossible things you would do or beating drums*

*of your past achievements to not feel your absence*
*in the circles you live; there is nothing to give*
*to this amount of barter, in which hard work is the only starter*

***so***

**If you loved the process of it, no matter what the drift,**
**you will pass it on, succeed, and be financially free.**
**It may not fulfill your greed**
**but only the need**

# another chance

**Someday,**
*We will give this another chance*
*To the space emptied to fill in*
*a relief to the stance*
*of 5 years standing and dreaming*
*good times with you at last..*


*Nobody would accept me*
*If it wasn't for you*
*Still, validation sucks, man*
*And I hate that*
*to the core, but that's not*
*a positive trait*
*That's what my self-help book*
*says, so have to swallow that*
*for the sake of consciousness*


**But you never saved**
*Neither my big messages nor my poetry*
*on your phone*
*Still, my dumbasses would ask you first*
*about the recent that I wrote*
*I called you my effing inspiration, man*
*and you got none.*

*There would be at least one*
*you would be proud to show off*
*Now I'm done.*
*And I know that "someday" would*
*be the afterlife*
*when the light goes off..*
*That would be my **"Prime Time"***

# have you?

***Have you ever*** *stared at*
*nothingness in a dark room*
*Why are you afraid?*
*if anything wouldn't bloom*
*And that led to a greater abyss*
*And now you are numb*
*and can even doom*
*the best relations you had..*

***Have you ever*** *listened*
*to the sound of silence closely*
*It's not just vibrations*
*I guess, surely*
*More often listening to it*
*gave me peace in my hard times*
*Now, earplugs are my best fit*
*putting them on*
*to listen to the voice of my own*
*crimes..*

***Have you ever*** *woken up?*
*and wrote a line*
*in your midnight sleep*
*that hit up your mind before sleeping so that you wouldn't forget*
*But still, remember it clearly as you sat*
*After being woken up*

*pieces of thoughts that poked up*
*your mind that this is dope & fixed*
*and write it as it is*

**I remember** *none of the poems on my finger*
*Tips that are lame but true*
*My subconscious would remember*
*as my conscience would shrink*
*updates/particular highlight*
*I hope I flew to the heights*
*Before losing everyone's sight...*

# everybody gotta

*everybody gotta friend*
*to talk over the weekend*
*I got pen and paper*
*to write for the weak hands*

*got some selfish bastards*
*sucking up my veins*
*& drain every inch of*
*glow, thrown up by the pain*
*shook them up to the core,*
*hop onto the board*
*to make them look bore*
*to laugh at the misery of all*
*one day for sure*

*not got an eraser*
*sorry I wrote it raw*
*IDC if you judge or find it flawed*
*coz*
*everybody gotta friend*
*to talk over the weekend*
*I got pen and paper*
*to write for the weak hands*

*I got best friends*
*who were first on my list*
*they got boyfriends now*
*I'm outta their list*
*so came up with*
*a trick to ignore*
*write and write*
*all blissful shit that u expect*
*but u don't know for sure*
*well*


*not got sympathy*
*or asked for it*
*everything is unaccepted*
*including your apology*
*for what you did*
*now I don't even recall your name*
*out of regret or shame*
*you were who again?*

*AND I SAID*
***everybody gotta friend***
***to talk over the weekend***
***I got pen and paper***
***to write for the weak hands***

# to all the exes

*__To all the ex-family members__*
*That lost*
*and those that made me tremble*
*a lot*
*Not just by their doings shrinkle*
*me the most*
*But just their simple thought*
*Cursing to most of them*
*to rot...*

*__To the ex-girlfriend__*
*about the regret that I chose*
*or the reason why we fall*
*and the reason to break loose*
*That I don't remember at all*
*Sorry for the slap, after which*
*I didn't even recall*
*My audacity to mention*
*you here*
*is just a misunderstanding*
*That went clear..*

*__To an ex-best friend__*
*Yeah! Right, you came to read?*
*Yes! I hate you a lot*
*and be free*

*to do some that's pressured on you*

*The reason for only hating you*

*from above them all*

*is because they took*

*Stand for me on the stage*

*when I needed them the most*

*But you decided not to..*

**So, the Last thing would be perfect to say**

**May God curse you for every friendship**

**"I must pray"..**

# the bird

*I wrote around 7 pages*
*and intentionally not save it*
*now writing this one*
*so that its ages well on the ages*
*fine would be too,*
*at least not regretful*

*to remember I stumbled on the edges*
*repetitive times I don't wanna recall*
*that I was an inch away, from the fall*
*every time pulled back by someone*
*or something uncalled for*

*Yeah, that someone could be you*
*a good friend of mine*
*don't remember the bird that flew*
*which flapped its wings*
*and told me to climb*

***The same bird mentioned above***
***got me every time***
***same god in the people I love***
***gave me hope to live for***

*same people I thrive*
*Yeah, I saw them as doves in*
*my mind aboard*

# waiting

*waiting for someone to call*
*trying to expect **1** at least*
*waiting for someone to recall*
*that I exist indeed*
*in this chaotic life of ours*


***2** Spotify playlists on loop*
*recommended podcasts on time*
*Listening to crap to shoot*
*the mind & life to grind on*
*What's achievable and prime*


*I left them on reading!*
*implemented for **3** days straight*
*Self-help books are bait*
*to follow some pre-described path*
*huh! is that even my grave?*


*finding reasons that life is not absurd*
*meaning to its meaningless nature*
*Reasons to live in **4***
*good deeds to die for*
*explanation to be rather inferred*

*Okay, now the time limit is gone*
*So far; no phone calls have shown*
*till 5 of the other day alone*
*nothing but probably grown*
*not us, but the distance from reality a bit more..*

# meet me

**meet me on a rainy day**


*I would strike my words*
*as swords to you*
*block them with your smile*
*just the way you always did*
*even if it doesn't fit*


*and counterattack when*
*The thunder blinds*
*for a second*
*I'll lose my guard in the meantime*
*Just make full use of it*
*Also, make sure to get a hit*
*as my three swords shine*


*This would be your last chance*
*just before my freaky stance*
*hard to read*
***tough vocab would***
***slash you in two***
*No Mercy! allowed to your plead!*
*and leave you perplexed*

*about how you lost?*


*And even if I miss the end*
*you would only get half the idea*
*how the sword curled back*
*and goes across your chest*
***Now, will you remember?***
*Every word for the best*
*and rest..?*

# for sure

***unusual places are peace***
*I may have been depressed*
*or full of anxiety in the places*
*people I went with considered beautiful*
*and heartwarming and all*
*but I felt at peace with the kitchen floor*


*I told myself about my adventures*
*of being alone, of being at home*
*I went back and forth in the stories*
*singers try to portray on the canvas*
*of mine that was not meant for display*


*repeating the songs in my head*
*to assure me*
*Do I really like the song*
*I heard at 2 a.m. or I was just sad,*
*and vibing to every other sadist thing all along*


***wrote***
*My most real feeling without being high*
*that I'm thankful for with a sigh*
*My best lines in the worst places*

*at least not where I dreamed poets would write*

*wrote my corniest line*

**"All the people I read and listen to are dead, and that's what makes their**

**art more unintelligible and comforting at the same time."**

*and I still quote my favourite person's lines, which were pure*

**"You will get through one of them."**

**one day! That's for sure..**

# counting the peace out

*it's ironical*
*how do I write the most depressed sounding*
*poetry through these glitter pens*
*They get through the most beautiful minds*
*Whatever way they comprehend*


*__one said__ it was cool another one felt sorry*
*one wrote and continued my poetry*
*through some lines that were unrelatable at the time*
*__a couple__ blessed me to rise and shine*
*asked me about writing a __book thrice;__ like I never considered it*
*I reacted shook and said Nah, man I probably would*


*yea! I acted surprised for the __fourth time__ in my entire life*
*coz every repetitive shit I have to act nice*
*I can't be rude and proud to talk about the future __high fives__*
*They would give me the __sixth book__ and call it "mine"*


*Whatever the experience, she won't even take good criticism*
*will ignore it while listening to __a septet__ until my one ear burns out*
*and will shout to them at quarter __past eight__*
*"bye-bye, baby, its been a sweet love" and leave it to fate*
*that my poetry grows in them until they understand*


*__Nine nights__ spent, only with some naps and cough*

*You will get one if you were close enough*

*My fantasy is to print **about 10***

*will talk about it to no one; be silent and pretend*

*as a secret*

**with peace, this piece would be the end..**

*To all the readers, thanks for being out there and reading my book. I hope this piece of my work led you to the emotions I portrayed in the process of coping with most of them by writing them out.*

<u>**May you find something new every time you re-read it.**</u>
*"No man ever steps in the same river twice, for it's not the same river and he's not the same man." — Heraclitus*

<u>**Don't forget to recommend and share it with your peers!**</u>

**Any query, review and criticism by any of you readers would be highly appreciated!**

**Instagram Handles-**

**@yaar_yogesh / @05_a_cursed_love_10**